Tips from your Property Shopper

SELLERS...read this!

MARGO LENMARK

*Many thanks to my friend, my partner,
and my lawyer, Steve Berndt
for his invaluable input and meticulous
attention to detail!*

About the Author

Before her move to North Carolina, Margo journeyed from her Midwestern roots to many parts of the U.S. and the world. In 1996, she visited Blowing Rock, and the beauty of the Blue Ridge Mountains so captivated her that she put down roots in this area. She became the sales manager at a high-end resort in Boone, and then started her own real estate company, Lenmark Properties, in 1997. She is currently a top producing broker with Blowing Rock Investment Properties where she fervently introduces clients to the beauty that allured her many years ago.

Remember these
four must-haves in the
mountains:
Good tires,
good brakes,
good cell reception, and
4-wheel drive.

FOR SELLERS

HOME | LAND OR LOT

Enjoy building your dream home in the mountains!

SELLERS...read this!

EXPENSES

Perk (if necessary), road maintenance agreement (if necessary), survey (if there isn't one), any loan expenses (if you are getting a loan), and attorney fees for closing are all expenses you should plan for.

Honey, here's how we shop your property!

DEED

Read the deed to find out if there are any restrictions attached to the property. Developments will have restrictive covenants. Make sure to read them, so you understand the requirements to build, the design guidelines, and the rules and regulations.

SELLING YOUR HOME

There's a psychology to selling. REMOVE THE OBSTACLES. When a recruiting firm recruited me years ago, I had many objections. *"I don't want to be in big group meetings."* You don't have to attend. *"But I don't want to move."* We'll move you. *"I don't want to have to find a place to rent."* We'll find you a place. With all my objections removed I ended up taking the job, watching them pack the moving van, and move me into the new apartment they found for me!

So let me help you remove the obstacles.

DISCLOSURES

Ask the seller for any pertinent documents or disclosures so you understand the property.

If in a development, speak with the Home Owners Association (HOA) president and get a copy of the restrictive covenants and design guidelines so you understand the requirements to build and the associated costs. Ask about the financial solvency of the development. Find out what the HOA fees cover and if they will increase once you've built your home.

PRE-INSPECTION

Hire a home inspector to inspect your home
and then have everything fixed on the list.
This helps for two reasons:
1.) the buyer won't be scared off by finding
a laundry list of problems when the buyer
does their home inspection;
and
2.) it will give you, your broker, and your
buyer confidence in purchasing your home.
Remember first impressions
are paramount!

INTERNET

Find out if internet is available, what kind it is, and the speed. Internet may not be readily available where you're planning to build.

REALTOR

Pick the right real estate agent. Check out their company and their company's website. Compare with other company's websites and Internet presence. Remember the Internet drives the market today. Check out the broker's familiarity with the market, the area, your type of home and how it is selling. Look at other listings and photos the broker has done. Make sure you find your broker trustworthy and that there is a good chemistry between you.

ELEVATION

Understand the elevation of your land so you can anticipate living on it and what the weather conditions will be like. If there is a steep road to your property consider what that will be like in the winter. Consider if you have the right car for the property as you may need 4-wheel drive. I always encourage a 4-wheel drive vehicle in the mountains. If it is on lower flat land, check to see if it is in a flood zone. It floods in low lying areas in the mountains.

DISCLOSURES

There are two disclosures you are required to fill out in North Carolina.
1.) Mineral, Oil and Gas Rights Disclosure and
2.) NC Residential Property Disclosure. Fill out the NC Residential Property Disclosure carefully."No representation" is an option. However, I only think you should use it if it is in a rental program and you have not lived there for some time. Otherwise, "no representation" could be a red flag for the buyer.

TOPO

This is a topographical map that shows incremental changes in elevation. You will need to understand the lay of the property, where the driveway will go, and the house site. Seek professional advice from a builder, a land planner, or an architect.

DOCUMENTS

You have an obligation per the NC purchase contract to provide the title insurance policy and any survey to the buyer. Also gather up any warranties for appliances and fixtures, and anything else you have that is pertinent to the sale of the property.

SURVEY

You will need to know the boundary lines of your property. Your broker may or may not know where they are. They are basing their information on what the seller has told them and the seller's information may not be accurate. If there is a survey, you may need to hire a land planner or surveyor to flag the corners. If there isn't one, you will need a new survey.

ROAD MAINTENANCE

If you are not on a public road make sure you have a road maintenance agreement with everyone on your road. It will make it more appealing for the buyer to want to live there. It will also be easier for the buyer to get a loan.

ACCESS

Make sure you understand the access to your property especially if it is outside of the city limits. Is there a recorded right of way to the land and who maintains the road? Also check for a recorded road maintenance agreement.

DECLUTTER

Take out your personal items and pictures and get rid of a LOT of STUFF. Have your Realtor help you decide what needs to go. You need to have space for the buyer to imagine themselves living in the home.

WELL

You cannot make drilling a well a condition of the contract. Therefore, you will need to find out if there is sufficient room to locate a well on the property. Or you may look into the possibility of a shared well.

CURB APPEAL

Remember first impressions! Pressure wash
the house and decks, if necessary. Freshen
up inside and outside with paint, if
necessary. Either landscape or maintain
the existing landscaping. Clean the gutters,
sweep the sidewalk, clear your view,
tidy up!

PERK

Does your land or lot perk for the number of bedrooms you need? Ask the seller for the septic permit. If there isn't one you will need to get one. Go to the Health Department and get an application and follow the instructions. This could take up to two months. Make your offer on any property subject to the lot or land perking to your satisfaction.

PRICE

Do not overprice your home. It will go into broker's minds as overpriced, and will not be shown, and will sit on the market, and you will blame your broker. If you do not agree with your broker's recommended listing price, consider getting an appraisal. A bank will only lend on the appraised value. An appraisal is based on what comparable properties have sold for in the last six months. It doesn't matter what you think your home is worth; it doesn't matter what the broker thinks you can get for your home; it doesn't even matter what a buyer will pay for your home. What matters is the appraisal, and that depends on the comps. PERIOD. The appraisal is almighty. Beware of a broker that automatically agrees with the price you want without giving you comps. You do not want a broker who just wants your listing; you want a broker who will sell your home.

BUYING LAND OR A LOT

It is hard for most people to see the potential for raw land. You will need to learn to look through the trees to see if there is a view. The best time to see the lay of the land is in the winter when the leaves are down.

So let's go shopping!

PHOTOGRAPHS

This is hugely important. Check out the pictures on your broker's other MLS listings. A picture is worth a thousand words, so you know how important they are. How many times do we see dark or blurry pictures? Or a picture of just a corner of a room? How do those brokers ever get hired to sell a house? Make sure you get great photos, the best photos possible. Today they have visual tours and drones which are fantastic. However, they work better for larger homes and are an additional cost.

Now relax and go shopping for new furniture!!

MLS INFO

Once your home is listed, check the MLS sheet for accuracy. You may be liable for any misrepresentation.

EXPENSES

Cost of all inspections, appraisal and bank fees including origination fee (if getting a loan), due diligence fee (non-refundable), earnest money (refundable), and attorney fees are the expenses you can expect to pay.

In North Carolina, we have a due diligence period in which you can perform all of your inspections. Sellers may require a non-refundable due diligence fee to take their property off the market while you do your inspections. You will also deposit an earnest money check in your lawyer's trust account. You will get your earnest money back if you change your mind within the due diligence period.

MARKETING

Have your broker send an email blast to all brokers in your area once it is listed in the MLS. Discuss the value of social media. If your home is high-end, you may want to do a visual tour. Call your broker and give them any ideas you have that may help sell your home. Working together can work miracles! Once your home is listed in the MLS, it will automatically go on Realtor.com as well as many other websites. Understand that Realtor.com is the only website that is directly linked to the MLS and therefore has accurate information. Many sites pull information from sources other than the MLS and may have inaccurate information. There is very little that your broker or their company can do to control that.

INTERNET

Check on internet availability. Believe it or not, there are places in the mountains where internet service is not available. If the seller says it is, find out the provider, what type and speed it is. Call the provider and double check that they will service the house.

ATTITUDE

Don't take any buyers for granted. This is a big step for them. The easier you can make it for them the better the experience will be for all. Make it a win-win. Be gracious. Don't mistakenly think that another buyer will easily come along. They may not and often don't for a long time. Weigh the odds. You may need to cut your losses and move on. Try to make it work with the buyer you have. Remember, "A bird in the hand is worth two in the bush."

HOME WARRANTY

You may want to purchase a home warranty for peace of mind. It lasts for a year and covers appliances should anything break.

CLEAN

Make sure you have a professional come in to thoroughly clean the entire house both at the time of listing so it will show well and at the time of sale. Any buyer wants to walk into a clean, beautiful home.

HOME OWNER'S ASSOCIATION

If you are buying in a development, speak with the Home Owners Association (HOA) president so you understand the development, it's rules and regulations, and what the HOA fees cover. Get a copy of the HOA restrictive covenants. Ask about the financial solvency of the development so you feel comfortable buying in the development.

EXPENSES

Getting the house ready to list, all agreed upon repairs, attorney deed preparation fees, commission, and deed stamps are all expenses you will need to pay.

SURVEY

The seller may or may not have a survey of the property. It is the buyer's responsibility to get one if they don't. Even property located in developments may have survey issues, so buyers may still want to have their lot surveyed. Do not count on your broker to know where lot lines are. Often the sellers don't even know.

FLOOD ZONE

Check to see if the home is in a flood zone and requires flood insurance. Yes, it floods in low lying areas, even in the mountains!

Enjoy the last days in your home, and prepare for your next adventure!

*"Dreams are our only geography—
our native land."*

– Dejan Stojanovic

CHIMNEY

If the home has a fireplace, have a chimney sweep check it out for function and safety. You may wish to change from a wood burning fireplace to a gas fireplace or vice versa. That change can generally be made by contacting your propane company.

SELLING YOUR LAND OR LOT

It is difficult for most buyers to visualize raw land. You need to take out as much of the guesswork as possible for the buyer. Just like you need to remove the obstacles for home buyers, you also need to remove the obstacles to a lot or land purchase. Here is how you will do it. It takes a little work, but it may save you months or even years of aggravation over trying to sell your property.

PESTS

Have a pest inspection done. Although termites are rare in this area, they do occur. There are also other types of wood boring insects such as carpenter ants and old house borers. The inspector will look for signs of infestation or damage to the structure by wood-destroying pests. If there is a problem you will need to have it treated. Ask if the seller is already treating the home for pests.

PERK

Get it perked for at least three bedrooms. That involves getting an application from the Health Department and following their instructions. You will need to prepare for the perk test by having holes dug so the Health Department can come out and test the soil. This can take up to two months.

HOME INSPECTOR

Find a good, reputable home inspector. The home inspector's warranty limits their liability to the cost of the home inspection. Have the home inspector check for radon. Radon is prevalent in these mountains. Get it checked! It is a leading cause of cancer but it is easily mitigated. We live in a temperate rainforest so test for mold. It too can be mitigated. Call the home inspector after the inspection and find out what the big concerns are if any. Ask the inspector what issues his inspection didn't cover. i.e., did he go up and look at the roof? If he suspects a problem, he will refer you to a roofer, an engineer, an electrician or some other appropriate professional. Read the NC Residential Property Disclosure CAREFULLY. If there are places where the seller checked "no representation" ask why. Investigate. However, there are reasons the seller may check "no representation." They may not have been there for many years.

BOUNDARIES

Many of you have no idea where your property lines are. If there has been a survey in the past, hire a surveyor to flag the corners, so brokers and buyers can clearly see where the boundaries are. If you don't have a survey, you may want to get one. Otherwise, the buyer will have to, which is an obstacle.

ACCESS

Check it! If you are not on a public road, you should have a recorded right of way. Also, check for a road maintenance agreement. We live in the mountains, so visualize the road in the winter. Ask what kind of maintenance they do. If Joe down the street plows the roads in the winter, what happens when Joe moves? Understand your access and your maintenance.

PREPARATION

Put in a driveway, or at least a path where the driveway will go, so buyers can walk to the house site. Clear the house site if cost is not prohibitive. At the very least clear the underbrush away and flag the corners of the house site. Take the guesswork out for the buyers. You need to help buyers see the potential for your vacant land.

SEWER/SEPTIC

Check whether it is a sewer or septic system or if there is a septic easement. Check the septic permit from the Health Department to determine the size of the system. Find out if the septic tank has been recently pumped. If not, you may want to have it pumped in order to check the tank. Older homes are especially problematic. The older septic permits did not require repair field areas, and there may not be sufficient land for a repair area. Septic systems are not built to last forever. But some septic companies have ways to repair old drain lines.

VIEW

Clear a few trees so the buyer can see the view if there is one. If you don't want to take the entire tree down, then at least remove some of the limbs.

WATER

Check water quality and quantity. If it's a gusher don't worry, but if it's a trickle make sure there is enough. Contact the original well driller to determine the number of gallons per minute. Between the date it was drilled and today it could have changed due to changes in the water table. Check water quality especially if it is near a Christmas tree farm. You may need a state test which is more expensive but more thorough.

INFORMATION BOX

Have an MLS sheet in a box on the lot so buyers can see the details. Have a copy of the survey of the property in the box, especially if it is acreage. If no survey, then place an aerial tax map in the box.

LAWYER

Lawyers close real estate transactions in North Carolina. Find a lawyer who specializes in real estate and is reputable. Ask for recommendations from your broker or friends who have used real estate attorneys in the past.

ACCESS

If you do not have public access, make sure you have a recorded right of way. Also have a road maintenance agreement in place if there is more than one home on your road. Not having one will most likely discourage a buyer, and it is not their responsibility to get one.

CASH PURCHASE

There are two things a seller will consider in an offer: Price and Terms. A cash purchase at the right price can be the winning ticket. Cash means the buyer will not need an appraisal which is good for the seller. If you study the comps carefully with your broker, you should have a good idea that it will appraise. Cash means that you can close quickly which is also very appealing to most sellers. Generally, the sweeter you can make the terms, the better it will be for the seller, and that may affect your purchase price. If not, it most certainly will make your offer more appealing than a financed offer.

INTERNET

Find out if there is internet service provided to this area and the cost to install. Internet is not available in certain areas in the mountains. Know your options so you can disclose them to potential buyers.

REALTOR

Find a good real estate broker. If you don't know any local brokers get a referral from someone you trust. Make sure your broker knows the market, has a good track record, and you have a good chemistry with them.

ELEVATION

Check the elevation and topography of the land. It helps buyers know how the land lays so they can plan their home accordingly. Also, check whether it is in a flood zone so you can disclose to the buyer if it is.

LOAN

Get pre-approved by a bank for the amount that you can afford. Sellers will take you seriously, and you will know for sure that you can buy the house. Shop around for different loan options and rates.

PRICE

Do not overprice your land. If you disagree with your broker, then get an appraisal for the same reasons listed under home sale.

There is so much to consider. You need to think through what is important to you.

The clearer you get on what you want, the easier it is for your broker to help you shop! Once you've found the property you want, here's what to consider next.

PHOTOS

Get fabulous photos if you can. When property is wooded, it is hard to get good pictures of it. But if you have a view, maximize it!

Do you want to live in a gated community? If so, what amenities do you want? What are you going to do with the property? Retire? 2nd home? Vacation rental? Many subdivisions have restrictions on short-term rentals and businesses. Obtain a copy of the restrictive covenants and determine if they allow whatever it is you want to do.

If you are building out of the city limits, you need to drill a well and perk your land for the number of bedrooms you want. You need to consider the cost of a foundation on sloped property. Most people want streams and views, but you usually can't have them both together. The best view lots were sold a long time ago, so if a beautiful long range view is important you may have to buy an older home and renovate it. Consider the amount of sun your land will get if you want a garden. When buying acreage in the mountains you sometimes only get a house site, the rest of the land slopes down the hill and may not allow much of a yard.

MARKETING

Have your broker send out an email blast to other brokers in the area when your land is listed. Speak with your broker about the best ways to market your land. Sometimes it is good to advertise in land magazines (especially if it's a large tract or unique) but often it's not worth it.

BUYING YOUR HOME

There are many things to consider when choosing to live in the mountains. You need to think about what is important to you. View, streams, privacy, gated community, proximity to town, amenities, acreage, farming, gardening, kids in school, access to sports activities such as skiing, hiking, swimming, canoeing.

Do you want to buy a home already built or do you want to build your dream home? Home or condo? Acreage or lot? Higher elevation and cooler or lower elevation and warmer?

DISCLOSURES

You will need to fill out a Mineral, Oil and Gas Rights Disclosure. If you are in a development, you will also need to fill out a Home Owners Association Addendum. Make sure to include the name and phone numbers of the president and the treasurer of the Home Owner's Association (HOA). The buyer and the buyer's lawyer will need these numbers.

Honey, here's how we shop for property!

MLS INFO

As with a house sale, check to make sure all of the information in the MLS is correct as you may be liable for what you represent in the MLS.

BUYERS...read this!

EXPENSES

Perk test, land preparation, road maintenance agreement, attorney deed preparation and any other closing fees, commission, and deed stamps are expenses you may need to pay.

FOR BUYERS

HOME

LAND OR LOT

Now, think about how you will spend your money!

About the Author

Before her move to North Carolina, Margo journeyed from her Midwestern roots to many parts of the U.S. and the world. In 1996, she visited Blowing Rock, and the beauty of the Blue Ridge Mountains so captivated her that she put down roots in this area. She became the sales manager at a high-end resort in Boone, and then started her own real estate company, Lenmark Properties, in 1997. She is currently a top producing broker with Blowing Rock Investment Properties where she fervently introduces clients to the beauty that allured her many years ago.

"We need the tonic of wildness... At the same time that we are earnest to explore and learn all things, we require that all things be mysterious and unexplorable, that land and sea be indefinitely wild, unsurveyed and unfathomed by us because unfathomable. We can never have enough of nature."
– Henry David Thoreau, Walden: *Or, Life in the Woods*

And *THAT* is why we move to the mountains!

*This book is dedicated
To all you lovers of Nature.*

Welcome to the unfathomable beauty of the North Carolina Mountains.

Tips from your Property Shopper

BUYERS...read this!

MARGO LENMARK

www.ingramcontent.com/pod-product-compliance
Lightning Source LLC
Chambersburg PA
CBHW061431050726
47593CB00006B/2309